This journal
belongs to:

_____

We would love to hear from you. Please connect with us to share your stories, experiences and photos, and to find many free resources.

{
🌐 www.PurpleSplashStudios.com

✉ Books@PurpleSplashStudios.com

f Facebook.com/PurpleSplashStudios

📷 Pinterest.com/PurpleSplashS
}

ISBN 13: 978-1977504425   10: 1977504426

What is a bullet journal?

A bullet journal is a customizable organization system.
It can include your to-do lists, calendars, doodles, memories and much more. The dot grid pattern helps guide drawing and writing.
Ultimately, it is a tool to help you reflect and get stuff done.

♡

A note for gymnasts / coaches

Bullet journals make a great tool to help organize your life at home and at the gym. We love gymnasts so have included some ideas and templates just for you.
Feel free to visit www.PurpleSplashStudios.com for more inspiration and to print out ready-made templates.

If you love this journal, please take a moment to review it on Amazon to help spread happiness and inspiration.

Ideas

Bullet journals can be used for many things.
Here are a few ideas to get you started.

Personal

- ☐ Calendar
- ☐ Important Dates
- ☐ Birthday Lists
- ☐ Appointments
- ☐ Weekly Chores
- ☐ To-Do Lists
- ☐ Fitness Tracking
- ☐ Water/ Food Tracking
- ☐ Habit Tracking
- ☐ Meal Planning
- ☐ Recipes
- ☐ Shopping Lists
- ☐ Vacation Planning
- ☐ Books to Read
- ☐ Dreams and Goals
- ☐ Budgeting
- ☐ Bucket List
- ☐ Party Planning
- ☐ Study Notes

- ☐ Doodling
- ☐ Diary Writing
- ☐ Memories/ Scrapbooking
- ☐ Gratitude List
- ☐ Affirmations
- ☐ And Much More

For Gymnasts/Coaches

- ☐ Goals and Goal Tracking
- ☐ Rehearsal and Meet Times
- ☐ Choreography
- ☐ Music List
- ☐ Inspiration
- ☐ Gymnastic Terminology
- ☐ Class Planning
- ☐ Attendee Lists
- ☐ Class Rules/ Procedures
- ☐ Student Information
- ☐ Motivational Quotes
- ☐ And Much More

Templates

Here are a few ideas for inspiration.

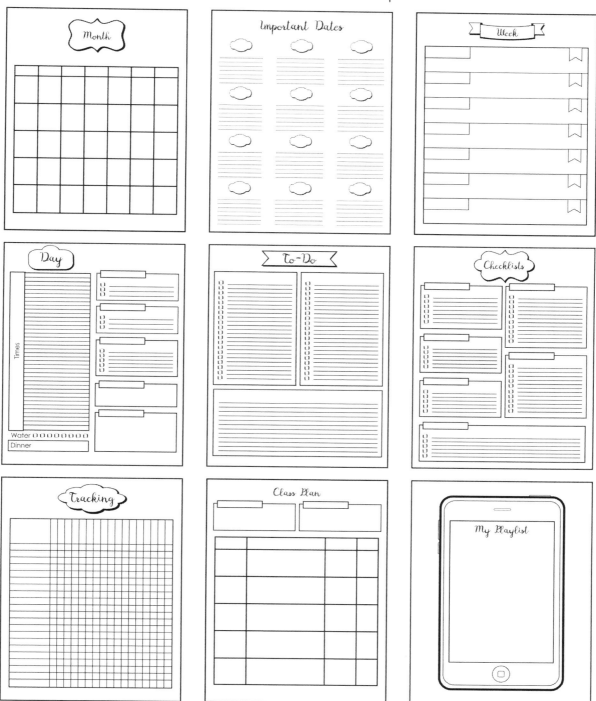

You can download these and more on www.PurpleSplashStudios.com.

Border Inspiration

Bullet journals can be as creative as you like.
Borders are a great way to add fun.

Doodle Inspiration

Here are some fanciful doodles to add some flair.

Key

Example

- ☐ Task
- ● Note
- ○ Event
- ★ Priority
- ◉ Explore
- ! Inspiration
- → Task Migrated

Index

Happy Journaling! ♡

Made in the USA
Lexington, KY
09 December 2018